From #dataleaks to #consentdata

beginning

the journey

toward

a data-centric

society

CONTENTS

"CONNECTING THE DOTS" SERIES

In my business activities, and even before in politics, sales, and during the compulsory service in the Italian Army (Artillery Specialist group at a Divisional level, within a mechanized artillery division), I often ended up doing just one task: connecting seemingly unconnected "dots" (people, information, resources, etc.).

The aim? To present the results to a non-specialist audience, thereafter acting as an interface, communication channel, facilitator, negotiating between multiple parties, usually to help first identify a target destination and pattern for change.

To steer the organizational ship (be it a small team, or even just an undecided individual) to the intended destination.

This usually involved a lot of reading, listening, thinking, and... "thinking as if I were wearing somebody else's shoes"- before writing.

Until a decade ago, these "connecting" activities weren't visible online, also if I had registered my first domain (prconsulting.com) in 1997.

This "connecting the dots" series, started in 2014, has just a common thread: repeating that "connect experience and knowledge to initiate change" approach, but focusing each time on a specific issue.

As my other online publications, these short books will be mere stepping stones toward further, longer books and new online/offline initiatives (e.g. management workshops, multimedia).

No, this is not just a "business methods" book, and does not want to be yet another addition to your "business cookbooks collection".

If you visit my Linkedin profile (address provided at the top of this page), you can find a link to a short trailer for my YouTube channel on change, ChangeTheRulebook[1].

It is just a "placeholder", akin to what you do when playing the game of Go (Weiqi) to "mark the boundaries of your intended territory", but it should give you a hint of what I am currently preparing.

Therefore, if you are curious or would just like to receive a list of links to articles online where I discussed those experiences, contact me, or otherwise use the "search" function on my my website https://robertolofaro.com.

You can reuse the material contained here, online, or in any link to my previous (or future) writings that I will provide you, either directly, or openly accessible.

---

[1] https://robertolofaro.com/ctr-channel

There is no limitation: if you think that it is worthwhile, you can also build up your business around that (as some consultants, university professors and political or marketing operators did in the past).

But you are to quote the source, so that others too could derive from my material without having to pay a derivative author (you) "royalties" (including seeming as if they were copying you) for what you didn't originate in the first place.

If feasible, add also a link to the original material, and send me a copy of your derivative material, and let me know if you would like it reviewed.

Previous volumes of the "Connecting the dots" series:
1. #SYNSPEC
   XXI Century Expert Team Building and Management
   ISBN 978-1499798074
2. #QUPLAN
   A Quantum of Planning
   (includes a 200+ pages fictional case study)
   ISBN 978-1508673422
3. 25 years of lessons (and counting) on relevant data
   ISBN 978-1496073594
4. Just another book on innovation (in Italy)
   ISBN 978-1723163937

A summary and tag cloud of each book is available on my website, along with links to additional material[2].

---

[2] https://robertolofaro.com/books/business-books

FOREWORD AND WARNING

The first volume of this series, released in 2014, was focused on collecting knowledge and allow those that are recognized as "experts" to interact with you, both in your personal and business life.

The aim is to improve your ability to obtain the best of both worlds: doing what you do with your own resources, involving those (internal, external) specialists if, when, and for how long needed.

This volume instead focuses on the impacts on social and business culture of our increasingly data-centric society.

It all starts by connecting and expanding threads discussed in three other books, published in 2014 (on BYOD), 2015 (on business data), and 2018 (on GDPR), as well as another volume on talent management, published in 20141.

The first step? Asking questions- just one question: considering where we are now, what could happen next?
And how can we influence the path?

Evolving into a data-centric society implies connecting a bewildering array of technologies.

Anyway, moving forward requires doing what we did with telephones, cars, TVs, and now smartphones: citizens and businesses have to develop a level of awareness of the potential and impacts of all those technologies- and their impact on everyday life.

Billions of people around the world are replacing everything from a watch to a banking account or a compass with their mobile phone.

In the process, they are scarcely ever switching it off- and each generation of smartphones gets more features (and sensors) than the previous one.

Up to the point where a smart device (phone, tablet, etc) is exchanging data via the Internet almost 24/7.

In my country, Italy, maybe even two or three for some, as there are more mobile phone SIM cards than inhabitants.

If you blend that trend with the increased urbanization, moving forward requires reconsidering many elements that we take for granted.

It is not just about technology, or about data privacy, our current, transient media-fed obsession.

In few years, we will talk about data following another paradigm.

As it will be basically impossible to have an ordinary life in our urbanized world without renouncing not just to data privacy, but probably to a degree of "mental privacy".

It is about a different role for citizens in a different kind of local and national, supranational, or globally.

In this book:
1. "Why #ConsentData" – the logic behind the title
2. "Your village is a wormhole" – new data citizenship
3. "Moving into a GDPR era"- what happens when a regulation delivers a degree of social engineering
4. "Connecting the dots" – future threads.

More material (e.g. updates, case studies, links, Q&As) will routinely appear online (please refer to my Linkedin profile).

1 WHY #CONSENTDATA

Data- everybody assumes to know what the concept means.

Anyway, also in business, what "data" means depends on who you are, as others might consider what you treasure to be just background noise, or even a nuisance.

A data-centric society implies that data are accessible anywhere, anytime, by anyone, and that there are compatible concepts of data (otherwise sharing data becomes impossible).

Moreover, that the time to actually set up or execute a transaction is almost irrelevant.

Scaled down by the amount of data exchanged and speed of connections that are available with 4G and will be soon common with 5G, mere dozens of seconds would be too long.

When you use your smartphone, do you really need to know how each component talks to each other, and how your smartphone connects to others via the network?

No, not really- pretty much as you do not need to know how to build a fridge to use it.

Moving onto data and access to data: simpler and more accessible than it was in the late 1970s, but we are still not there.

You do not need to think, as when I started working in the late 1980s, how to connect with a central system.

Or, as it was before the mid-1990s, to use an external tool to transmit data to a central storage system, so that it could be delivered to another computer at a later stage.

Amazon with its AmazonWebService[3] and others created additional services using their platforms to build their own offer.

E.g. Google[4] already has a "pay-as-you-use" platform of pre-configured services, as do others, e.g. INTEL[5] and MICROSOFT[6].

The common point? Moving from having a software development team build up something for you, to having an architect pick up components from a toolbox and then a smaller team (or just a software) focus on "connecting" everything.

But, if compared with the 1990s, you do not need to hire people able to do that- it can turn into a "pay-per-use", a variable cost.

When we talk about "data" and "consent" within the same phrase, it is better to consider our starting point.

Somebody will say that, after the computer age, we are now firmly into the Internet age, and starting to turn into the age of the cloud- computers are everywhere and nowhere.

But, on the data dimension, in just few decades after the WWII we had huge changes.

XIX century: imagine that you are coordinating the movement of a fleet.

Your communication means? Light and sound- e.g. flag signals (e.g. have a look at movies showing communications during the battle of Trafalgar)- as it had been done for a while.

Jump to the 1990s: *"The advent of the modern microprocessor has completely changed the situation. A processor such as an Intel Core i7 with 4 cores clocked at 2.7 GHz is just as powerful as the supercomputers of the 80s. Hence, it is now possible to computerize critical on board functions such as control, guidance, navigation, and collision avoidance. In particular, the development of digital FBW (Fly-By-Wire) systems has revolutionized the operation of both military and commercial aircraft."*[7]

A similar quote could be added for cars, or any other kind of modern mobility vehicle.

---

[7] Antony Jameson, "Computers and Aviation", page 9
https://pdfs.semanticscholar.org/87d2/6915cd56c3dbc1a557919a675803d8b7469c.pdf
(retrieved on 2019-01-13)

What happens when you bring on board computers? Your generate and log data- and then a whole industry builds on doing analysis on those data.

Having data available implies also that new standards of compliance will be enacted upon them.

Now, consider that for drones new rules have or are being defined, as traffic control for thousands of drones would create an amount of data exchanges on the coordination of the occupation of airspace.

It is not just a marginal increase in the number of flying objects to control, is an increase of few orders of magnitude, also because they can take-off and land anywhere.

I will discuss other examples in the last chapter.

The common concept is: we are so used to data, that we cannot even consider that, until WWII, anything was still done mainly by hand or using mechanical calculators.

Sometimes, for critical tasks, this implied having multiple people doing the same computational task, and then compare: as did the onboard computers of the Space Shuttle.

So, we were actually surrounded by data well before the smartphone, as microprocessors were in widespread use for decades before even the slow 3G started operating.

With each generation of storage support (paper, punched cards, magnetic tapes, etc.), we had a significant increase not only of data that could be stored and transmitted, but also the issues that this generated.

In paper-based times, leaking information implied having access to e.g. a camera.

In computer and cloud times, there is a constant stream of massive leaks: from losing USB keys containing the data of thousands of individuals in UK, to wikileaks, Panama leaks, and a continuous stream of data losses from various services online.

When there are massive data leaks, you never know if they are real or intentional (done in order to phase out something).

It could be considered that also some famous financial data leaks were actually useful to force a change in regulations in some jurisdictions, changes that most certainly would not have happened, were to be subjects to e.g. a democratic vote.

In our computer and increasingly cloud world, the issue isn't about storing and transmitting data- is about keeping track of further reuses and transmissions.

There are some social consequences when moving into the cloud era- we need to adapt our customs to our current inability to keep track of all the uses of information (albeit technologies such as blockchain and Edge Computing and cloud might, combined, provide some help in the future).

Personally, as I was born in a company town, I do know that "privacy", and "confidentiality" are relative values.

I find quite entertaining when somebody from my hometown talks about "consent" or "privacy" when referring to access of personal or business information.

By inclination, a company town is a "closed environment", akin to closed cities during the Cold War[8].

"What happens in Las Vegas stays in Las Vegas" probably was never really true, if you had reason to hunt for information, but nowadays is simply impossible.

It is a sign that exposure to Cambridge Analytica, Snowden, etc. are actually increasing awareness about the issues of data ownership and data privacy/confidentiality.

A welcome development, as the forthcoming role of cities in the XXI century will require, to thrive, to be part of the global community.

It is actually a case of market (re)design- something that delivered a Nobel Prize[9].

When you design a market, you also have to consider the distribution of information.

Unfortunately, the key issue is that this requires a cultural transformation, something that implies accepting the temporary rebalancing of the pre-existing roles.

We are currently able to collect, store, transmit more data more often than even before in human history.

Therefore, it is just delusional to be able to do what was common until before the Internet era: selective leaks.

---

[8] "Closed city" https://en.wikipedia.org/wiki/Closed_city
(retrieved 2018-12-29)
[9] Alvin Roth "Nobel Prize Lecture"
https://www.nobelprize.org/prizes/economic-sciences/2012/roth/lecture/

Many years ago, when we still used typewriting machines, it was common, for confidential pre-release documents, to type different variants: add a typo here, change a word there, whenever there had been a previous leak e.g. to a competitor or to the press.

Reason: to track down the source of the leak.

In a data-centric future, each data transmission will be a transaction with a potential economic/relational value.

Introduction

Since the late 1990s, by identifying what I focused on (content and presentation, plus limited components to store and distribute data), I was able to delegate everything externally (in Canada, in my case)- also if the size of my team varied from one (most often) to few people and representatives of other teams.

But you still had to do your homework on what you need when.

And, if you wanted to have your own central data storage and processing, you should hire full-time employees able to continuously monitor operations, and fix a variety of routine issues and minor/major crises.

It is similar to something I saw in a previous "professional life", between the end of the 1980s and the early 1990s, on "Computer Aided Software Engineering" (CASE).

CASE tools promised to bring an "assembly line" approach to software development- e.g. the ability to reuse components developed by others.

The difference now? Most of the main players listed on page 2 deliver a degree of "free" or "test drive".

Also the smallest company can build up innovative services for free, hiring no IT experts.

Involving instead an innovative but technically adept web agency to do the job (they will usually have their own roster of software experts).

Maybe transferring then the results to another company that will monitor and maintain it in the most efficient way, and routinely adding more innovative people from other web agencies.

Aim? To jointly review suggestions for improvement (as originators focus mainly on incremental innovations).

The few paragraphs above actually might seem "cryptic".

A proof that, no matter how "simpler" things are made, there might still be the need for few layers of "intermediaries".

Call them technology experts, business experts, integrators of business and technology, solution architects, or whatever is trendy when you are reading these pages.

This is just to show that we are at a preliminary stage in our data-centric society- the concept is still a bit exoterical.

In 2019 already Android and IoS cover most of the mobile market and enable any user to simply add any application to a device that is becoming an extension of each user's body.

What is still missing is a Lego(tm) box of tools and a common parlance, in plain English- a "lingua franca".

With a device, smartphone, car, and soon any ordinary appliance and accessory (yes, including your clothing), anybody will be both a data producer and data consumer.

The old "demand and offer"- simply, extended not just to those willing to incorporate, but to anyone, anywhere, anytime, and always "on demand".

Jump few years in the future.

If your sunglasses and clothing were to need to adapt to the external environment...

...why should not collect information from the environment where you are heading to?

And then report back (suggest or even decide) which "configuration" would be more appropriate for you?

Almost three decades ago, a book talked about how advances in manufacturing would enable mass-production car makers to introduce an era of mass customization.

Then, few years ago it was said that advances in genetics would enable mass-production of customized medicaments.

So, why not think about any mass-produced product to turn into an on-demand, individually designed product: clothing, food, mobility in urban centers, and any accessory or device?

A mass-market of individuals with individual needs (e.g. some would tolerate more light) would actually create demand for services we cannot even think about.

The funny part? It will be akin to going back to the customization level available in pre-industrial times.

Back then, most had home-made clothing and food.

This time, will be done by machines (assisted by people or software, and integrated with communication channels), and continuously adapting based upon your own use of products, services, and interactions with others.

Each time what belongs to you will access information, data exchanges will happen.

We do not need to look into a more or less distant future.

If you look e.g. at your Android smartphone, it carries along a wide range of sensors for various purposes.

Maybe in part originally designed for functional purposes, e.g. avoiding excessive heat that could damage the device.

Or for specific uses, e.g. to allow playing games with your smartphone without having to use any external device.

Or even to enable extend the level of services, e.g. the NFC that enables payments and other forms of transactions.

Or features that evolved, e.g. the camera that now in some countries is often used also to read QR codes and complete cash- and creditcard-less financial exchanges.

But what is already happening is something else, as your smartphone, being embedded in your everyday life, is becoming part of your activities (albeit sometimes it seems as if you are becoming part of its activities).

And there are also applications that enable the digitalization of real-world objects, e.g. by printing a form and then taking pictures, so that the an application can create a digital model without the use of any external equipment.

But the activities listed above include a degree of explicit consent: what if it that consent were to be instead "derived" from your actions?

Of trends and facts

As written above, we consume and generate data-continuously.

First and foremost: you probably read a lot about "consent" in articles concerning data privacy as well as blockchain.

In this book, the former is more relevant, but, in later sections, also the latter will be involved.

Therefore, the relative/subjective concept of "need to know" will have to be completed with "right to know" plus a "data access agreement".

Not just because it is required by the GDPR, but simply because a data-centric economy attaches value to both information and its uses.

It is akin to what happened within the art industry: long ago, you would buy a painting of a sculpture, and it would be yours.

More than a decade ago, a family friend who had an art gallery told me that with contemporary artists it was common to have included within the sale of an art object only a limited set of reproduction rights.

E.g. just for the catalogue page, to avoid the resell as t-shirts, posters, or in videos, with additional costs for even a reuse for the cover of the catalogue.

Moving or evolving into a data-centric society implies a cultural change and a long list of technologies.

Obviously, this applied also to previous innovations, e.g. the introduction of personal computers.

But if you carry around a smartphone or tablet, you know that data are exchanged continuously.

When I refer to "smartphones", think to any device that is mobile or contains an element of "intelligence", an ability to collect, process, and distribute data.

Soon, you will surrounded by devices that could be classified as having enough "intelligence" on board to be able to carry out those tasks.

So, a change of times- and let's look at a current technological example

.

I often use Googlemaps (it replaced my GPS gizmo that I had over a decade ago- one battery less to keep charged).

Few months ago, after I saw that anyway my new smartphone was suggesting itineraries and shops based upon my previous visits, I activated the visibility of the tracking information known to Google.

Not only I can see only part of the information that, instead, is blatantly available to Google itself.

But when I was in buildings for a while, first as a kind of reverse privacy I could see slightly off-the-mark information (e.g. distances and timing).

Then GoogleMaps started asking confirmation of where I had been within the building.

We are both consuming and producing data- continuously-and you feel almost guilty when not providing information that, frankly, is totally irrelevant for you.

There is a difference between you and Google- or Apple or other vendors that are creating their own "ecosystems" on top of their devices, i.e. really "economic environments centrally controlled by them".

You have to "pull", or explicitly request most of the information you want, except when notifications are active; in the latter case, you receive information when specific events happen (and even when you do not really care).

Instead, your counterpart continuously "pulls" information broadcasted from your device, either by sending it online, or by storing the information on your device, and then extracting when needed.

This has obviously some side-effects, including companies that developed technologies extracting that (and other) information from your device.

Technologies that supposedly they then were unable to control, as shown by various scandals.

Not just the usual suspects- also software companies working for security forces worldwide "leaked" information, through hacking, disloyal employees or simply failure in managing security, including an Italian company.

Another element worth considering is the timeline of response: your device is able to receive and answer requests for information much faster than you will ever be able to process (i.e. to give your consent to).

An interesting feature of the GDPR, the EU data privacy regulation whose "transition period" ended in May 2018, is that implicit consent, as routinely done by websites and apps that used to pre-fill access authorizations, is not acceptable anymore.

It is actually part of the "privacy by design" and "privacy by default" presented by the GDPR.

Now, that is still a work-in-progress, as I saw on two of my Italian mobile phones: when I visit a website from a supplier website, I get onto another website without even a single warning, and instead of having by default disabled consent on "value-added" services that self-activate via full-screen advertisements and link to your mobile phone credentials, I had to do the opposite of what GDPR implies.

Or: I had to contact each individual operator to decline consent.

Imagine if that were to be applied to all your future Internet-enabled clothing and devices.

Yes, we do need to extend the GDPR "explicit consent" approach to each and any IoT (Internet of Things) and Internet-enabled device.

In my view, also on blockchain.

Either I am made aware, when I use a blockchain, that all those then accessing it will see all the "history" of the information, or there should be a "decoupling" of information, i.e. storing on the blockchain just keys, and having the data whose key is on the blockchain elsewhere.

You could retain the "tamper-proof" and "distributed" (i.e copied across the network) features of the blockchain, while retaining data privacy on the content.

But more about the blockchain later.

Or: "ask only what you really need to provide the service the user is asking, and, in absence of consent or in doubt (e.g. changes), do not access information you have not been explicitly authorized to access".

Since May 2018 I tried often to review the authorizations requested e.g. by apps or websites using another website (Linkedin, Twitter, Google, Facebook, etc.) to avoid having to re-register with them.

As, luckily, beside my mobile phones, all my devices and computers are re-routed through them, and, for the time being, I do not think (but I may be wrong) that I have other Internet-enabled devices on me.

Well, if I ignore the NFC-enabled credit cards that, if unprotected, could actually authorize small (25EUR, I was told) transactions just by proximity, no signature needed.

Again: is that something that would require consent?

Many websites have removed the request to authorize access to third-party personal information unneeded to deliver services e.g. access to your list of friends, when you just wanted to see the weather.

Anyway, many still pre-select options, and a few still add authorizations that are somewhat quixotic, and beyond the scope of the application.

The more the data and the higher the frequency of access to data, the more difficult is for us humans to filter.

Or: to really provide "informed consent".

At least, "informed consent" at the same speed required by the system to process data only in that moment and only for that purpose, as noted above.

For example, consider instead of GoogleMaps one of the many apps that list restaurants or hotels: why should you register just to search a list?

In most cases, the concept is a quid pro quo (you give something to get something).

But it is almost never a transparent negotiation, e.g. less data for less features or additional costs, as you do not have access to the list of all the details that are transmitted.

Actually, sometimes I was talking with various types of users, from digital natives to digital enthusiasts to those refusing using any kind of "always on" technology, while they were registering on websites or apps.

And, again, saw that the well-meaning "consent" of GDPR has been turned into a business opportunity: to obtain access to data that they did not ask before.

Some apps on Android and some websites actually went a step further, making quite cumbersome the "onboarding" (your registration), i.e. starting to add so many steps, that in the end most users simply click OK to each request, without reading the "contract".

If each app were to be requested to list the individual data items that they will access, and how, when, why, and for which part of each specific service, would anybody bother to read?

If some privacy advocates were to "fight" for that right, it would be just an ego-trip for the advocate (and maybe a stepping stone toward a political career), as it would have no practical value.

And this is exactly the reason why "privacy by default" and "privacy by design" are two of the most important features of the GDPR, features that will support the development of a working vendor-independent ecosystem for a data-centric society.

In China currently not having a smartphone is starting to become impossible, if you live in major towns.

Even cash is not used anymore- cash has been replaced by a QR code on WeChat[10].

---

[10] "China's obsession with QR codes"
https://technode.com/2018/02/16/photo-chinas-obsession-qr-codes/
(retrieved 2018-12-29)

Components and their stakeholders

Therefore, we need another approach to "informed consent".

The starting point?

Consider data as part of transactions, each one involving different parties with different interests, motivations, and roles within each transaction.

A digression on the concept of "stakeholders" within a data-centric environment might be useful.

In a "data-centric" society, you are expected to spread data continuously.

If you are to build a society on that concept, you have to consider your own data production as more than just "data".

You could have agreements to share all the data, part of the data, and both across time, e.g. all the data all the time, or part of the data part of the time (more about this later).

Delivering something isn't enough: you have to consider also how to counterbalance potential negative impacts for part of what you are delivering.

Moving onto the "data" domain.

If you are familiar with the basic concepts of privacy, the data that you generate might have impacts on others.

E.g. by disclosing information about yourself or your consumption patterns, you might disclose somebody else's.

19

For each data "component" (or data element, if you prefer), you have to consider who and how will be impacted, and which level of "licensing" (or "consent") would be needed.

It would make sense to convert your smartphone into your own secure "personal data licensing central".

Then, you would need a way to express consent on a transaction-by-transaction basis, but at the same speed of the interactions requesting that consent.

Your smartphone could actually become your own "personal gateway", where also information for anything that you buy should transition and be "licensed" to interested third parties, before they can access it.

The simplest and most user-friendly option would be simply to admit that no mere human would ever be able to ensure that "consent" can be delivered instantaneously.

If we are really to enforce strict compliance to the concept of "get only what you need, when you need, and for what I asked to do- no more, no less".

"Consent" implies also a "reasonable retention time" for data- data stay no longer than they are needed.

Then, the next step would be to force mobile phone and other mobile device suppliers to "unbundle", and open access to the information that they store on mobiles.

There is a further element worth considering.

Are we increasing the amount of data that we are "broadcasting"? Most certainly the answer is yes.

Over 50% of the Internet traffic is now on mobile phones[11].

And via other mobile devices, e.g. on board computers on cars, or non-computers, smart TVs and various devices, or the like of Amazon's Alexa.

But, with 5G and other high-speed Internet options, we will have more options to spread data locally, wherever we go, and geographically.

It is not just the quantity, but also the level of detail (granularity) and quality (type, frequency, correlation, etc.)

The point in marketing was never just to sell what you had- but to produce what could be attractive to customers.

An increase in data quality therefore implies how deep what is shared goes toward the ability to actually forecast your behavioral patterns, and anticipate or create needs.

Yes, we are back to 1920s "Propaganda", but within a continuous dialogue between suppliers and customers, mutually influencing each other.

Your mobile devices can track so much data about not just what you do, but also how (e.g. eventually the use of the camera to analyze your facial expressions) and, of course, when.

---

[11] "ITU estimates that at the end of 2018, 51.2 per cent of the global population, or 3.9 billion people, will be using the Internet."
https://www.itu.int/en/ITU-D/Statistics/Pages/stat/default.aspx
(retrieved 2018-12-28)

This is the list of activities related to physical properties that an app called "Physics Toolbox Suite" can do on my mobile:

g-Force Meter	Magnetometer	Tone Detector
Linear Accelerometer	Compass	Oscilloscope (Audio)
Gyroscope	GPS	Spectrum Analyzer (Audio)
Barometer	Inclinometer	Spectrogram (Audio)
Roller Coaster	Light Meter	Multi Record
Proximeter	Color Detector	Tone Generator
Ruler	Sound Meter	Stroboscope

Think about your mobile device as a "correlation device": so many details, that while maybe it is too early to have a cause-and-effect analysis on events as they unfold, a continuous re-assessment of correlations becomes possible.

Moving then eventually, when you have enough data, from correlation to causation.

When most objects will have a short-range Internet connection, it will not make sense to transmit centrally all the minutiae.

Do you think that the details on how many times you opened for how long your fridge should be transferred to a central server of your white appliances supplier?

Maybe those data could interest your local supermarket, to offer you discounts tailored to your consumption.

Say: smaller rations, different packaging, etc: prepare for sensors analyzing what you put in your trashbin to identify waste and suggest improvements to you purchasing habits.

But, again, will need consent.

Just placing an RFID or other sensor and track it, as it was done in the past, would not be "consent"[12].

Unless... shops will start asking to sign a consent on each purchase- the higher the number, the less chance that customers will give a "conscious consent".

On the business-to-business (B2B) side, it is actually increasingly common for companies to exchange more information with their suppliers, notably for larger companies.

Of course, if you have a factory, instead those data may actually interest the company that provided the power generation equipment or tools for your production lines.

Some companies already moved from "selling" into a "pay per use" model, for something as small as tools to be used at a construction site, and up to power stations or heavy machinery.

Again, too much data dropped just into what is called a "data lake"[13] would not add value- just consume resources.

I saw already in the past few decades in management reporting activities, adding more data could actually be useful just to... obfuscate the data that you really need.

Our brains aren't wired for a continuous stream of largely meaningless data- we are inclined to "filter out".

---

[12] E.g. have a look at how much what in 2014 was considered almost science-fiction is now reality- https://robertolofaro.com/byod (apologies for the self-citation)

[13] https://en.wikipedia.org/wiki/Data_lake (retrieved 2018-12-29)

Soon maybe even full factories (would make sense e.g. for forthcoming remote 3D printing facilities scattered close to the customers, but pre-built as even thousands of years ago Carthaginians did with for seafaring activities).

Therefore, the more the data, the more interest in deciding which data should be collected and transmitted as they are.

Sorting out which should instead be stored locally, and transmitted only "on demand".

It is a form of "management by exception" (e.g. when something is not working correctly), or after some "transformation" (e.g. aggregating, removing identification data, integrating with other local classification information and cross-references to a shared taxonomy).

It is part of what is called "Edge computing"[14], another application of the principle "think globally, act locally".

Furthermore, we are increasingly becoming more urbanized, and our towns will often turn into places where most people will spend all their everyday life.

Including by gradually reducing mobility with private vechiles to leisure, for most.

We will be able to work from home or from local co-working facilities shared by many companies.

And we will probably move around mainly with shared or "on demand" mobility vehicles coming to our door.

---

[14] https://en.wikipedia.org/wiki/Edge_computing
(retrieved 2018-12-29)

Unlike current co-working facilities, probably these offices will have higher flexibility (e.g. the possibility to set up a teleconferencing or virtual presence meeting room at short notice, with dynamically rearranged sizes according to demand).

Even mobility vehicles might be completely different from what we are used to now, e.g. storing on your mobile phone your configuration parameters.

When the vehicle comes to your door, or you will pick up from the nearest parking slot (as it is already feasible now), it will be actually configured via software as if it were your own.

For the time being, the game is "improving the efficiency of mobility", but probably in few decades the point will be not just about speed, but about efficacy: less travel but more efficient for few people.

For some activities, it makes sense to have faster travel, including e.g. by enabling to spend a week-end on the other side of your continent without getting on a plane.

But in many cases, e.g. for back-office employees, could make sense both to have them work from home, or "teamwork" when needed from a meeting room that in reality does not exist (i.e. a virtual meeting room- 5G will allow a different kind of "telepresence").

If people will spend more time closer home, probably there will be more data exchanged and integrated with other local data.

And more apps that actually interact with other apps, creating a local "data oasis".

A treasure trove of closely correlated data across a long span of time, that will enable other kinds of marketing.

This implies also reconsidering the role of the "individual transportation" device par excellence, i.e. your car.

Think for example to traffic lights, e.g. as shown by a test on technologies to remove traffic lights.

And letting instead cars "talk to each other"[15]: it is an example of collaborative behavior that only a data-centric society would enable.

A data-centric society enables also a "smarter" approach to the use of resources and consumption.

It is already becoming commonplace to have tax credits or even "metering at the delivery point" (e.g. for garbage collection) for a variety of social behaviors.

From reducing the waste of food, shortening and coordinating supply chain routes across multiple companies at a town level, to cross-scheduling the use of infrastructure.

Including the local electricity and communication networks, to the actual allocation of road and parking space.

Therefore, we will have to choose between giving blank consent, or having something smarter (or at least faster) than us making decisions, decisions on which data to share when, and with which other third-party, including opportunistic one-time partners.

---

[15] Ozan K. Tonguz "Red light, green light- no light", IEEE Spectrum, October 2018, page 24-29, http://spectrum.ieee.org/v2v1018 (retrieved 2018-12-28)

Maybe the next step would be to have on the market apps that allows users to self-profile just once, by answering a questionnaire.

And then use the profile built through the user's answers to decide instantaneously if a data request from an app makes sense or not, and asking the use to "manage by exception".

Or: contact the user only whenever there is a case where an activity requires an additional authorization that, based upon the profile, would not be acceptable.

Nothing so innovative, if you think about it.

It is akin to regulations requiring that customers of a bank or another financial institution have a profile adequate for the level of risk embedded within a financial product.

The main difference?

This assessment will be done at the end-user side, and continuously.

Expanding also the user's privacy, as the providers of each app delivering such a service could be required to provide just that service: we had in the past regulations for other professions.

Removing conflicts of interest should be associated with structural separation.

We all know what happened when "Chinese Walls" like post-1929 depression regulations were replaced by less stringent requirements and self-regulation.

If you blend technology with the contraction of distance and increase of potential interactions in urbanized environments, you are moving toward a different social structure.

In our case, a social structure where technology is embedded within everyday life.

And where fine-tuning of all the interactions between technological infrastructure and humans will require even more data: acquired, exchanged, processed continuously and locally, defining then a "circle of influence" licensing.

As any sub-community, not just each individual, will have an infrastructure to use locally the data in order to plan, improve, and optimize services- and exchange that information with higher-order communities.

Imagine a future world where each major town will be producing and consuming locally everything, from equipment spare parts, to produce and electricity.

In a data-centric society, most of the maintenance and distribution activities that are currently done by people will need no human intervention.

Because those activities are either predictable, or associated with specific "signals" that would allow e.g. an automated dispatch of a "pre-emptive repair" team.

At least from 2010, and installed from 2014, there are technologies that allow e.g. to disable a power line when interrupted.

So fast that the interruption is identified even before the ruptured cable touches the ground[16].

A technical detail? Not really- as the technology enabled e.g. Iceland to improve its power distribution and increase its stability.

And to fast switch on and off a circuit without generating disruption is a critical element for the integration of inherently unstable power sources (e.g. solar and wind).

Also, this would allow to e.g. use future fuel-cell cars as temporary electricity storage facilities when parked, to manage demand.

As an example, see a 2016 article on the subject[17].

Aiming to have self-sustainable towns does not imply getting back to the Middle Ages: we live in an interconnected world, and data can travel at the speed of light.

So, we have to reconsider also what does mean "local" and "national", if we want to extract most of the potential benefits of a data-centric society.

---

[16] "Synchrophasor Applications in Transmission Systems" https://www.smartgrid.gov/recovery_act/program_impacts/applications_sync hrophasor_technology.html (retrieved 2018-12-28) and and Peter Fairley "Utilities roll out real-time grid controls", IEEE Spectrum, October 2018, pag 9-10, http://spectrum.ieee.org/utilities1018 (retrieved 2018-12-28)

[17] "Reverse mode fuel cells for energy storage" https://iecetech.org/Technology-Focus/2016-02/Reverse-mode-fuel-cells-for-energy-storage (retrieved 2018-12-29)

2 YOU VILLAGE IS A WORMHOLE

In the previous chapter rephrased the concept of "consent".

As for the title... let's say that you can read a definition of "wormhole" online[18], but it is a shortcut to visualize a concept.

Let's say that a wormhole is, in the end, a "connecting channel" linking distances that, if you were to move in a line from A to B, would take forever.

If, instead, you "fold" the distance between you starting point A and ending point B, so that they are one above the other, A is actually just around the corner from B.

So, A can influence B and viceversa, as they are in a kind of "line of sight".

---

[18] "What is a Wormhole?" https://www.space.com/20881-wormholes.html (retrieved 2018-12-27)

Now, leaving my distorted perception of science-fiction and physics, we can visualize that in our own world.

Distances are not "folded" as in the title of this chapter, but actually made continuously shorter by telecommunications and transportation systems.

In barely a century, we moved from horses to planes to high-speed trains.

Soon probably we will have the hyperloop, a concept that, when announced, reminded me of a 1930s science-fiction movie about an underwater train connecting continents.

Then, maybe we will have also in a couple of decades an elevator bringing us into orbit, and even sooner we will be able to have a vacation on the Moon.

Down to Earth, a constellation of satellites is making instantaneous communication possible anywhere in the globe (the last country joined the Internet few years ago).

Furthermore, there are now multiple global positioning satellite constellations in orbit: beside GPS for the USA, following a denial of access a while ago during a conflict near Europe, the EU has its own, and Russia and China too.

Before starting, let's see on the next page how the diffusion of the Internet evolved, worldwide, between 2008 and 2018[19].

---

[19] https://www.itu.int/en/ITU-D/Statistics/Documents/statistics/2018/ITU_Key_2005-2018_ICT_data_with%20LDCs_rev27Nov2018.xls

As you can see from the radar chart, it is not a matter of expanding the use of the Internet, it is also the variety of the channels: fixed, mobile, broadband, radio, etc.

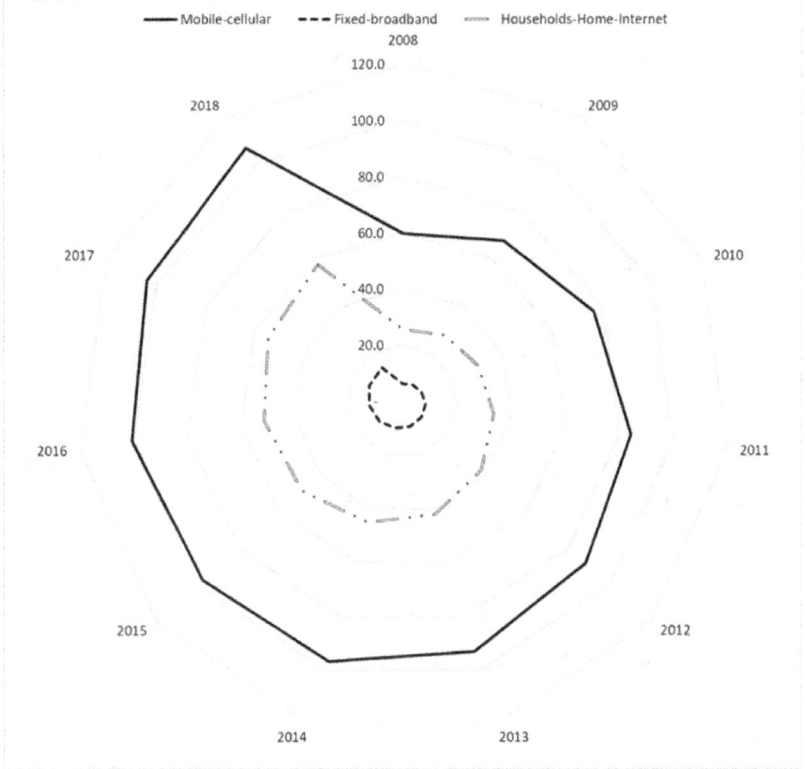

I highlighted just three elements, as "mobile-cellular" is now showing in many countries (mine, Italy, included) that users have more than one active data connection (myself included), generally one per device they routinely use.

And this will become increasingly common in the future, when Edge Computing and the lowering in size, cost, energy consumption of device will make possible disposable Internet-capable devices embedded into any object that is made by human or machine.

Then, we will have, as discussed in the previous chapter, to consider how to aggregate consent at different levels.

GDPR is not the only regulation defined by one national or supranational entity that applies globally.

Think about anti-money laundering, or trade agreements: they are still managed often as bilateral agreements, while those targeted (individuals and companies) increasingly operate at a global scale.

Sometimes the discussions about the future of human communities (e.g. urbanization exceeding soon 70% of the Earth inhabitants) seem focused just on defining a different, more local approach to control.

As if suddenly all our towns were to turn into a self-contained city-state, with the local authorities adopting an imperial status.

Actually, even already existing city-states are more integrated within the global economy than most major cities in existing countries founded in the XIX century.

It is certainly true: re-importing in town activities, notably those that had been for a long time "outsourced" outside towns (e.g. food production), could actually require redefining both the physical and social structure of the town.

Without going back to Thomas Moore "Utopia" and its distribution of roles within the community: a data-centric "smart city" could deliver more services with less social control, in no small measure thanks to the automation of most of the activities that Moore assumed were to be part of the social duties of each citizen.

Smart cities filled-up with sensors, cameras, and citizens with their own smartphones, and cars or mobility vehicles sharing data with each other.

Therefore, just to manage traffic or pollution will require a different legal framework.

Within the European Union, GDPR and, say, VAT, already imply that the rules of the Member State of the end user/consumer side increasingly do apply.

GDPR applies to anybody dealing with European Union citizens, wherever they are.

As you can see from the previously shown radar chart, it is not just a matter of expanding the use of the Internet, but of what this implies.

Internet, in most EU Member States, is not a "local" communication channel, i.e. there isn't a single "central information exchange" filtering access e.g. to the Internet in other EU Member States (with an exception, adopting a concept similar to the one followed by China).

Also if instead a centralized "filtering" approach was true for data-centric systems designed and delivered in the 1960s, e.g. the Italian central risk databank (Centrale del Rischi, first active since the 1960s).

Or, to stay always in Italy, the TV rating system called Auditel, activated in the early 1980s.

But still adopting a 1960s concept (i.e. a meter installed in few thousands of households and providing information to a central data collection, storage, processing point).

Currently, a small company specialized in just one activity can be embedded in multiple supply chains involving different companies based in different countries.

In the future, faster communication networks and faster and more convenient transportation will generate data across communities, data that could actually be useful to improve the management of resources of any town aspiring to become a "smart city".

Data that will be actually carried around by those involved in their generation.

But, as discussed in the first chapter, distributed data implies that collection, storage, processing will be actually done at the local level.

Many consider that this will happen for technical reasons (e.g. even with 5G, transmitting centrally all the data and video feeds that will be generated locally would be impractical)- Edge Computing as a technical solution.

Personally, based upon past experience on the evolution of data processing at different levels and with different architectures, I think that eventually business purposes will be the main driver in "selective unbundling" of data.

There will be data that, by consent (from individual) or consensus (from multiple parties), will be stored in the Cloud.

But for most of the continuous stream of data generate and transmitted, it would make sense to keep them locally.

The GDPR is generating within the EU a cottage industry of service providers "solving" GDPR issues.

Frankly, most are adopting an old approach to data management: collect, store, process/transform, distribute.

Or: a centralized data store to collect all the information from all the sources, as a central gateway.

Now, move five years into the future.

At least in my knowledge, none of the solutions currently is able to process and re-route in real time all the volume of data that will be spread around by our sensors that we will carry around, from sensors in our environment, and by the interactions between all the parties.

It is true that sometimes old solutions solve new problems, but the previous chapter rephrased, indirectly, also the concept of "location" and "roles".

Look at our current economy: Uberization[20] is transforming the concept of ownership of physical objects, so imagine what could happen with data.

Most of the personal cars in towns currently spend most of their time sitting in parking slots- when we will have fully automated vehicles, even those buying their own car might "lease" to Uber and the like their car as a personal additional revenue stream while they are e.g. sitting in their office, or sleeping at home.

Data will be your own property that you could share, and turn into a revenue stream worth of Walter Benjamin, i.e. a single set of information redistributed multiple times in various aggregate forms, generating multiple micro-revenue streams.

---

[20] https://en.wikipedia.org/wiki/Uberisation

We could have data-only companies that would aggregate and disseminate data, and there are already proponents of services, ranging from blockchain-based secure data storage on your mobile, to central data storage, to an Italian company whose claim was to be nothing short of "revolutionary".

I am currently based in Italy, so I will try to give data privacy examples also concerning Italy.

In a previous book, on GDPR, expressed also my doubts about all those offering "anonymization" services.

While closing the first draft of this book, I read an article about such a service offered by an Italian company[21].

In their case, in effect the philosophy seems to be to deliver a XXI century version of the Italian system Auditel, set up in the 1980s to monitor a sample of families on their TV consumption habits, data collected in real-time.

In this case, they offer instead to receive authorization to represent customers, so that the company can contact companies collecting data, invoking the rights to access and portability that are provided by GDPR.

Will it work?

Well, good luck- as per GDPR, neither "right of access" nor "portability" are a continuous, real-time affair, and it is not free forever.

---

[21] Weople, l'ad Siliprandi: "Con i nostri dati non diventeremo ricchi. Ma possiamo fare la rivoluzione" https://www.lastampa.it/2018/12/29/italia/con-i-nostri-dati-non-diventeremo-ricchi-ma-possiamo-fare-la-rivoluzione-mLE8Tdwrahl6aL17uLUgFl/pagina.html (retrieved 2018-12-29)

Read it again the GDPR: if you keep asking for data, you can be charged a reasonable amount (of course, if the first answer did not contain the data that you asked for, then that could be considered a violation).

So, if in the 1980s they had to provide a device to install in your home and then poll the data, now they offer to let others pull all the data, then become involved as a middleman, and share the proceeds.

There are further points that, just by reading that article, I consider significant commercial weaknesses of the approach, but I will let you make your own mind.

Also SAP announced a way to ensure that data cannot be referenced back to individuals.

Nonetheless, if you "enrich" data by cross-referencing with other data sources, even if all removed identification information, in the end you are profiling: and you are delegating your data life to a third party.

Why? If you remove identity, but then cross-reference ("augment") across enough factors, you close on those individuals fitting all the parameters.

As I was told half-jokingly one year ago for a potential contract: they were looking for an Italian speaking fluent French, English, Italian and used to work in a specific field with a specific set of experiences in Italy and abroad- there weren't that many.

In a true data-centric society, you do not need anymore "central providers", as infrastructure will, in reality, increasingly become a "common".

What we need are shared approaches to data distribution, not shared intermediaries.

Cloud computing isn't just a way to reduce investment for companies.

Anybody can have access to communication and computing infrastructure on demand, they just need a device to connect.

Anybody- including start-ups, corporations, and individuals.

Let's get back in time, before moving forward.

From 1920s "propaganda" to mass-manipulation

Probably the most famous "old" book within the PR and marketing industry is from the 1920s: "Propaganda"[22].

A famous marketing quote from the XX century? "Half the money I spend on advertising is wasted; the trouble is I don't know which half.", but somebody in 2016 said that probably that was an underestimation[23].

Post-WWII we got used to mass-production, mass-media, and generally "broadcasting"- including advertisement, and therefore measuring results implied checking on the receiving end, and making assumptions.

Social media online obviously changed all that- hence, proposals to actually collect data generated by users and provided to their suppliers.

Anyway, also without intermediaries, if you used anything from Amazon to Facebook to Google since, say, 2010, you know that increasingly what you do affects the advertisements that you see, and viceversa.

Reportedly recently Facebook experimented with another approach: altering the news feed "emotional tone".

You have always to take for a pinch of salt anything about uses of online communication.

---

[22] https://en.wikipedia.org/wiki/Propaganda_(book)

[23] https://www.forbes.com/sites/georgebradt/2016/09/14/wanamaker-was-wrong-the-vast-majority-of-advertising-is-wasted/

Aim: to identify correlation between actions.

It seems that altering the newsfeed "emotional" content had a side-effect on the ensuing communications, at least at a level that was noticeable.

It is anyway, the concept of "influence" (and "influencers"): it is not just outright advertisement, but also communication that results in having those receiving it heading into the desired direction.

The supposedly more precise online advertisement could actually represent a distorted perception of reality.

Your advertisement might be clicked not for a real interest, but for a temporary, "influenced" tunneling of the interactions of a group of users.

Whatever results in terms of conversion into purchasing could not have a causal relation with how good your campaign was- but of... how good the convergence of other "influencing" campaigns with your own was.

So, if you consider how easier is now to influence with a "burst" of focus, the assertion that advertisement online is significantly more measurable than its traditional counterparts, might be a case of narrow mindedness.

You can get a precise count of your own "internal events" (number of clicks, etc).

But does that really counterbalance the geometrical increase of the number of potential further factors?

And does that give any hint of which advertisement will work?

Disintermediation of communication channels (really?)

Maybe we have to reconsider what "freedom of expression" means on the Internet.

It is true that Facebook Instagram etc. enable person-to-person communication between many members of an audience, and it was interesting how this was approached by GooglePlus, with its "circles" approach to connections.

As I will discuss later, and hinted before while talking about "sub-communities" in a data-centric society, I think that circles are more appropriate to our data-centric future than other paradigms, and pulling off the plug from GooglePlus now might actually be a strategic move.

The fate of GooglePlus and other online experiments? Have a look at the GoogleGraveyard[24].

All those experiments confirm that, while the www invention was a way to disintermediate communication, social networks online (and many of the various "online ecosystems"[25] built by companies) are the XXI century equivalent of mainstream TV channels of few decades ago.

As each one of those ecosystems thrives only insofar its members keep contributing and connecting content.

Unique content?

Not necessarily- interactions matter as much as content.

---

[24] https://www.wordstream.com/articles/retired-google-projects

[25] https://en.wikipedia.org/wiki/Digital_ecosystem

Have you ever seen the movie "Black Hawk Down"?

It was a book and movie about some events in Somalia.

A side-effect of the war in Afghanistan (the invasion from USSR and the USA sponsoring of Afghan fighters) was the large quantity of Stinger left around[26].

Reportedly, in order to shut down an helicopter, an approach used was to "saturate" the environment with multiple launches, to deny access to airspace.

In IT security, there are similar approaches: taking over computers via a software, and then launching a concerted attack on a single computer[27].

As discussed for recent political events and ongoing campaigns, sometimes this kind of "saturation" is quite common in communication and "influencing" online- not just for political campaigns, but also to launch products and services.

The key element is, anyway, the availability of cheap and widespread continuous access to mobile Internet.

How many of you really switch off or, at least, set in "fly mode" your mobile at night?

---

[26] https://www.bbc.com/news/av/magazine-38808175/black-hawk-down-the-somali-battle-that-changed-us-policy-in-africa and https://slate.com/news-and-politics/2001/10/stingers-stingers-who-s-got-the-stingers.html

[27] https://en.wikipedia.org/wiki/Denial-of-service_attack#Distributed_attack

Prior to the GDPR, the main update to data privacy was in the 1990s- before smartphones became as common as doorbells.

Actually, more common.

Therefore, the Data Privacy Directive[28] wasn't "fit for business" in the XXI century, as it represented a different era.

Also, the old Directive did adopt, except for those few going around (at the time roaming wasn't cheap), really a country-by-country perspective (it wasn't a regulation, so it required a national implementation in each EU Member State).

Online, offline, many still consider the GDPR as "red tape" with no value added.

In reality, in some countries, most of the "new" rules supposedly introduced by the GDPR were already in place (also if compliance wasn't widespread)[29].

Data privacy in the 1980s and early 1990s, and therefore consent to use data, were mainly a one-to-one affair, i.e. in most cases the data provided by a customer would stay with the supplier, or follow a well-defined transmission pattern.

With Internet and http-related technologies, data can be transmitted, transformed, enriched using public channels, and e.g. already in the late 1990s a customer of mine was able to deliver to foreign banks in UK an Asset-Liabilities Management service with data exchanges via the web.

---

[28] https://en.wikipedia.org/wiki/Data_Protection_Directive

[29] https://robertolofaro.com/gdpr

Data exchanges in a wormhole society

When I started working officially, in 1986, we routinely used as sources books (including business and IT books) that were 5 or 10 years old.

Nowadays, it seems that most sources are what used to be called "instant books".

In reality, in our acceleration of knowledge transfer activities, often we lost depth- and it is now a routine to have long-term strategies... sent back to the drawing board even faster than in the old joke about the new CEO receiving three letters from his (as it is a really old joke- CEOs were just men, back then) predecessor.

First letter, first year, just one line: "blame me".

Second letter, second year: "it is your fault".

Third letter, third year: "prepare three letters".

In my activities mainly in change and management reporting and related projects or initiatives, I am used from the late 1980s to a much shorter cycle.

Or: in the first six months, in a complex environment, you can pick up "signals", but probably in many cases you will need some "local" to make sense- as you do not know the informal structure.

If you stick around after five-six months, you should have an understanding of the environment, its processes, its resources, and the real roles, not just the official titles.

In reality, what is defined "impossible to solve" often is just something that is cross-functional.

In almost thirty years, whenever there was something fitting that description, the sad reality often was that the bearer of the effort to solve it would not have reaped the benefits.

Therefore, if you are not just trying to cocoon somewhere, you can take the risk- considering that the benefits will be on the organization at large, and maybe if properly managed build "cross-functional credits" for the future.

But if you fail it will be akin to that second letter- and you can be much, much lower than a CEO or reporting to CEO, and still be "entitled" to the negative side of the consequences.

Now, six months seems to be a short time: but actually right now is the typical cycle of assignments on projects when you are supposed to deliver segment of a change.

Anyway, having an "operational" cycle of six months does not imply that everything has to be designed to be six months long.

In my activities in change, cultural and organizational change usually had a timeframe of 1-3 years, to produce results (was a function of scope, mandate, resources, degrees of freedom, etc.)

In management reporting, when implementing a new data-driven approach, usually it would have been realistic to assume a multi-year initiative composed of a first "foundation", and a continuous convergence and improvement, releasing something useful often (in some cases, it was an incremental expansion with weekly releases, in others a mix of timeframes).

Anyway, that was the "operational" side- but it was based on extracting knowledge and informal knowledge that wasn't built up in six months, or made obsolete in one year.

Over the last couple of decades, unfortunately often all around Europe I saw an inclination to reducing the knowledge content of activities- not out of need, but out of alignment of the mindset to the operational side.

Typical phrase: if it isn't solved in X, find a workaround- will fix it later.

Which really means: never.

It is becoming quite common: if an issue cannot be solved fast, it is ignored- until it moves from a routine maintenance of processes, systems, infrastructures, into an emergency (and in my country, Italy, this is sadly becoming a routine approach).

But this does not affect just physical or virtual objects: the most critical element, for now, is... humans ability to adapt.

The timeline for real change did not evolve- as our human brains do not really shed in few months habits built in years or decades.

Swapping technologies nowadays might take minutes, if your company or your supplier is using the cloud.

But swapping in your own brain the habits built over years might be something else, as shown by many marketing campaigns trying to "push" new versions of products- ranging from sodas to mobile phone or software interfaces (think about e.g. Coke and Microsoft Windows 8).

Since the late 1990s, and increasingly since the widespread adoption of smartphones, we saw repeatedly the "wormhole" approach in action.

Decades ago, we talked about the "butterfly effect"[30].

It is associated to the late 1980s book from Gleick on chaos[31], but in our case (data) focusing on characteristics associated with Mandelbrot's fractals[32].

In our future (actually, current) data-centric world, we need to get used to rely on "centres of excellence" in each and every domain of knowledge.

As in many communities I belong to that are linked to special groups or academic circles, we will get used to a "reliability scoring system", to solve another issue of our society post-WWII.

Visibility, what "The Century of Self" showed as a side-effect.

We had experts in A that were then called upon to provide their advice on B C D- and, in order to stay visible, they did so.

Some stating clearly what were the boundaries of their knowledge, but way too many eventually doing what they would have never accepted by their collaborators: making it up.

Add "philosopher" or "futurist" to your job titles, read just executive summaries, and you can be 24/7 in interviews, as a "resident expert".

---

[30] https://en.wikipedia.org/wiki/Butterfly_effect

[31] https://en.wikipedia.org/wiki/Chaos:_Making_a_New_Science

[32] https://en.wikipedia.org/wiki/Mandelbrot_set

At the time, there was a bonus: few would remember.

Internet and social networks online obviously changed it all: give now the same quixotic interview you would have given in 1990 on something where you have just an opinion, but leverage on your role of expert on something else to make it pass as expert advice- it will immediately backfire.

This will probably evolve into a "scoring" system that dynamically updates how worthwhile is considered what you say- depending on the domain.

For the time being, we can get back to old fashioned books that resulted from real research.

A good example of "old" approach is the collection of cases discussed within the 1990s book "Business Transformation Through Technology", containing 21 business cases across multiple industries[33].

It is a short book, but for each case presents the context and the approach followed to introduce change, and could help you in defining the stepping stones for similar studies.

The cases listed as part of the "Technologies for Business Processes" cluster are still available on the Cordis Europa website, e.g. ROCHADE[34].

---

[33] Rosalie Zobel "Business Transformatioon Through Technology", 1998, European Commission
https://www.librarything.com/work/22737513/book/164460409

[34] "Reengineering of complex aircraft development processes in distributed environments"

3 MOVING INTO A GDPR ERA

It is true that a couple of years should have been more than enough to harmonize data privacy laws (and associated compliance) across the EU.

As the GDPR is a European Union regulation, i.e. applies across the EU Member States.

The GDPR applies worldwide, if you want to deal with personal data of EU citizens.[35]

And fines, to get rid of the typical avoidance schemes, whenever applicable are on the worldwide turnover[36].

---

[35] GDPR is "on the protection of natural persons with regard to the processing of personal data and on the free movement of such data" (this is the official title of Regulation (EU) 2016/679)

[36] Cfr. Art. 83 "General conditions for imposing administrative fines"

But there are few further elements worth considering.

Italy is the usual suspect- I wrote in the past why we usually see compliance as something to do "on the last minute of the last day"- because it is not uncommon for laws and regulations to be changed, continuously and even retroactively.

Anyway, this time, we weren't alone, as it seems that many treated the May 2018 deadline not as the end of a transition period, but as the end of the beginning of a new one.

Some countries simply decided to drop the "fines" side, while overall you can still witness on a daily basis how companies all across the globe suddenly discover that they actually have EU citizens' personal, identifiable data on their databases.

From what I heard in Italy, even in official events about data-centric business, as of June 2018 most of State and local administrative entities managing personal data did not even have a DPO (Data Protection Officer).

And, from a quick check few months ago with colleagues, it seems that even the private sector was way behind, moreover if you consider how many of those newly bestowed the title of DPO had actual prior experience on data privacy.

As of December 2018, I was still routinely receiving GDPR notifications from companies that actually received the data from a third party, but never bothered to confirm that they had consent.

A different concept of market

The most interesting element of the future application of the EU GDPR regulation will be when data will actually be shared by individuals who will benefit from this data sharing, either directly (e.g. as micro-payments for sharing their own data), or indirectly (e.g. by off-setting the cost of a service, or gaining "credits" to be used toward a third-party service).

As all these transactions will be traceable, expect eventually also the taxation system to consider "within scope" also these forms of revenue (the grey area is significantly larger in an offline world).

Actually, as I wrote while still living in Brussels, a decade ago, it can be expected that eventually it wil be possible to have a continuous, real-time assessment of income taxes.

Back then, my suggestion was that, talking for example about my country (Italy) where a large share of businesses registered at the Chamber of Commerce in each location (it is compulsory) is too small even to be considered small, it could become feasible to drop the requirement to keep accounting books, and accounts could be directly managed by the State.

From January 2020, in Italy even shops that work mainly with cash will be required to report on a daily basis to tax authorities (from July 2019, only those whose income is above a larger-than-average threshold).

Now, as many in Italy say, that is currently set-up, as the universal e-invoicing that became compulsory from January 1st 2019, mainly as a tool for tax authorities.

Reason? Italy has an endemic issue with tax evasion.

But, in reality, Italy will be an open lab to define a new regulatory framework.

Our current fixation on data consumer vs. data provider therefore will become a false dichotomy.

The GDPR regulation has some reference also to "business models"- but, in the future, when most objects will collect and relay data e.g. about their usage, business models (and, therefore, data that are relevant) would change dynamically.

It is akin to the KPI concept: you can use a Key Performance Indicator as a target only until all converge on your objective.

Would you keep spending resources to continuously monitor something that everybody achieves at 100%?

Or would you identify some other "organizational behavioral change" to introduce on top of that, build a KPI on elements that allow to measure it, and monitor this new KPI?

If your data-centric business were to be built on being the only one able to provide a specific type of measurement, when others were about to produce different but equally useful measures, then probably it would make sense to develop something new.

There is no reason why a computer software able to improve e.g. the sequence of tasks involved into processing a paper or electronic form, cannot eventually lead to software controlling machinery and physical resources able to focus on the bottom line, and re-arrange how it uses the "inputs" to produce the "output".

Monitoring multiple signals that identify how competitors are operating, and where they could be heading to.

In this new "market"[37], data ownership should be directly linked to a "contract" associated with further constraints.

I might give my consent for purpose A within the an agreement to receive a service, with a specific business model that my supplier proposed when we entered into the agreement.

But also if the service received were not to change, a change within the business model of the supplier might require a confirmation of consent, e.g. with reference on how data can be stored, processed, "embedded" along with other data.

Example:
- you buy an ice-cream and subscribe for notifications about special deals
- now, imagine that the shop becomes part of a chain that sells also sandwiches
- you may or may not expect the data about your ice-cream purchases to be reused to identify which sandwich you could probably be interested to eat- and this is already within the GDPR.

But what if:
- the data are anonymous
- are used to indirectly identify which ice-cream customers should be targeted for other products?
- you might have signed up for marketing information.

---

[37] Alvin Roth "Who Gets What"
http://www.robertolofaro.com/books/suggested-readings/215-roth-who-gets-what-market-design-isbn-9780007520787-3-5-5

Also, if an individual were to voluntarily release information as open data, to be used anonymously, e.g. those provided by the sensors (s)he carries around (smartphone, smart clothing, accessories, etc.), other individuals passing by could rely on those data.

But what about the interaction between their sensors and the sensors of the other individual, influencing each other?

It is, within the physical world, a scenario similar to the one from the Facebook "influencing" experiment.

To make again an Italian example that is for now, not a distant future.

As discussed in a seminar on e-invoicing in Italy that I attended in late 2018, to ensure that invoices are considered relevant could imply to actually require/enable information about procurement- up to details on each line of each invoice, i.e. transmitting your purchase order and associated technical details.

Information that, in many cases, is business-sensitive- and released without a specific NDA or data-retention policies.

Caveat: as many of the clauses related to e-invoicing, and actually any Italian law, things might evolve, both toward a "smarter" and a "dumber" path.

As discussed above, making data "anonymous" doesn't matter that much if you then can cross-reference with other data that could "de facto" narrow down the number of potentially involved individuals or companies.

Need for a new trust infrastructure

I am not referring to blockchain.

We need a way to consider degrees of freedom, strengths and weaknesses associated with each data exchange, if we are to constantly share and transact data.

What we need is a new trust infrastructure, linked to our individual preferences.

Actually, it is nothing new: yes, GooglePlus (a.k.a. as G+) is closing down, a case of "controlled obsolescence".

But this happens when actually it makes sense to adopt the G+ concept of "circles" as a framework for our future "everybody is a consumer, everybody is a producer" forthcoming data-centric society.

Have you heard of "smart contracts"[38]? Currently, are associated with a form of blockchain.

The idea is that a transaction isn't just an exchange of value,

To make the concept easier to grasp: a transaction includes also conditions, maybe Service Level Agreements (SLAs), and other elements associated e.g. with the release of value as "automatically triggered" by a specific release of service.

Companies are used to the concept of "pricelist", linking a product or service not just to a value.

---

[38] https://en.wikipedia.org/wiki/Smart_contract

Usually, in business, a supply is associated to various conditions, e.g. the INCOTERM EXW implies some conditions of delivery and sharing of risk between customer and supplier, while FOB has other conditions.

You do not need to negotiate INCOTERM details, and apply worldwide.

E.g. my first comprehensive learning on the INCOTERMS was few years ago while getting through a course on... Mandarin in business- no, currently I do not have Mandarin language business skills, was just out of curiosity, for my future learning.

You need just to negotiate to which level of conditions you and your supplier (or you and your customer) will agree that the transaction has to be associated.

Now, move in a digital world- there are already some applications of artificial intelligence and machine learning to compliance[39].

Why should each transaction be negotiated ex-novo?

Why cannot you use the same "circle of trust" concept to automatically create "exchange arenas" that enable an exchange only at a specific level of conditions?

If your transaction is available, say, within the "FOB-data" type of circle, everybody willing to have transactions only at the "EXW-data" level will have to look elsewhere.

I know that this example is quite "Spartan".

---

[39] https://www.visualcapitalist.com/regtech-regulatory-risks/
(retrieved 2019-01-14)

Frankly, also whenever I was asked to design complex processes, workflows, or even organizational structures, I always adopted a Lego™ brick approach as a starting point.

Unbundle complexity, and identify its components, their interrelations and correlations, and the degrees of freedom needed (or available, in case of compliance).

Then, get something already existing and conceptually close enough, and build on that- as in most cases re-inventing the wheel makes sense only if you re-invent also the vehicle and the terrain.

In our complex world, most of the regulations and laws actually follow "patterns", i.e. nobody is so crazy to re-invent everything really from scratch.

Interestingly, as I worked cross-industry since 1986, I saw how often even those claiming to "invent" are actually adapting, consciously or not, what is already common in another domain.

Even funnier, when you can also "protect your intellectual property", by actually claiming rights to an innovation that is just a replication.

But this says more about our concept of IPR and patent or copyright, than about our brains.

Added bonus: if you "recycle" regulatory or process patterns, you can leverage and reduce resistance to change.

So, a good starting point to "regulate" data-centric transactions would be to take the latest INCOTERMS, and then start a Working Group on a new standard.

Actually, once developed, such a standard could become a "transactional chip" to be installed in any device enabled for data-centric transactions exchanging data for value.

For science-fiction fans: akin to Asimov's Laws on a chip[40].

No, I will not express my concept of "The Three laws of a Data-Centric Society", as I am quite confident that there will be plenty of consultants ready to write a "data-centric manifesto".

And we have already plenty of "replicants" developing manifestos, laws of this or that, and, in the process, creating a nice job opportunity for themselves.

Look at any technological trends: artificial intelligence, blockchain- there is no scarcity of gurus.

It is better, for the time being, to have each one of you think about what could be YOUR version of the three laws, and what could be the consequences on YOUR concept of a data-centric society.

Way too many consider the three laws of robotics at "face value", and not as a representation of an ethical framework, i.e. a choice of a behavioral model.

The idea would be to "embed" such a law-on-a-chip in any data-centric-ready device.

Meaning: any device enabling to be both a consumer and a producer of data with the associated economic transactions, smart contracts, etc.

---

[40] https://en.wikipedia.org/wiki/Three_Laws_of_Robotics

So, I would not be that much surprised if, after closing it down, it were to turn into a bunch of patents to be used for the next life of G+ as embedded within the AndroidSuite.

Maybe a chip with an API (Application Programming Interface) to actually generate a "mini-ecosystem".

To automatically enable data-centric transactions between devices.

Not just pre-defined transactions, as discussed e.g. in the Stanford paper I will discuss in the next section, but also, based upon the profiling of the individual, previous history, and proposals by interaction with other devices, new types of transactions.

As, in the end, it is nothing more than a more advanced and structural version of what you use with e.g. Bluetooth- only, in this case, what is transmitted influences the constraints based upon the specific "circle" that will be used.

If you are under 35, probably you are used to provide a rating to events, restaurants, cafés, shops. etc.

There have already been court cases sanctioning misuse of rating sites, but, as with advertisement, it is the same "saturation" issue.

When I started working, I wasn't working on audits, but my company was derived from that environment.

One of the issues discussed was "who audited auditors", and in companies that was turned into "who controls controllers": but in both cases it was a matter of few points of control.

After 2008, there were complaints about the role of rating agencies, and potential conflicts of interests, so much that other agencies were created outside the USA.

Also because this would allow to procrastinate, in some cases, the effects of automatic sell clause when going below a set rating- i.e. by having new accredited rating agencies counter-balance the vote of the usual three.

In 2015 I shared some ideas about the potential of rating agencies able to deliver on-demand an "instantaneous assessment" (e.g. a "SWOT"), by having just some "smart" pieces of data collection software accessing the public side of websites belonging to corporations and watchdogs.

Or: a "continuous profiling": obviously that was a joke- as we all know how inflated is information online.

Online anybody can issue a rating: who rates the raters?

Now, let's keep in mind that question, and move onto that 400 pounds gorilla lurking around us: blockchain.

I will not even bother to try to explain the concept behind the blockchain- there is plenty of free material around, and probably I can suggest a couple of references, but will use just the original paper[41] and the Ethereum book[42].

---

[41] https://bitcoin.org/bitcoin.pdf (retrieved 2019-01-11)

[42] https://github.com/ethereumbook/ethereumbook (retrieved 2019-01-11)

Why blockchain isn't a cure-it-all

While blockchain case studies promise full traceability, a real public blockchain has some characteristics ensuring that nobody has 100% control (well, actually 51% or more).

Most of those "business blockchain applications" that I keep reading about in magazines and newspapers, or somebody outlines to me are, frankly, a completely different beast.

Thinking in terms of business-to-business (B2B), consider the features of a blockchain listed by SAP in its own training on blockchain support[43]:
1 Multi-party collaboration
2 Process optimization
3 Security
4 Transparency and auditability
5 Information imbalance
6 Immutable digital assets

Does your project/service fulfill those requirements?

Most of the business projects that get so much coverage on newspapers aren't about digital assets.

And are often under the control of one single party, or even based on a centralized database.

Before getting carried away from one of the many vendors offering to solve all your organizational and systems issues in your company by using blockchain, think.

---

[43] https://open.sap.com/courses/leo4 (free online)

Do you really need a blockchain?

Or, maybe, you need just a centralized, shared database used internally, and consider also how much data and how fast have to be transactions.

I keep reading of "blockchain initiatives" that are actually nothing more than a QR-code on the packaging of physical products, pointing to a page within a centrally managed private website and database.

Basically, a central authority that we are asked to trust "by default", removing the "distributed" concept.

Shouldn't that "distributed" be a key element?

Otherwise, we can call "blockchain" any project using the old checksum (a kind of "digital fingerprint"),

What is the concept of "distributed"?

The reason why a blockchain usually is not appropriate to keep track of large volumes of data: whenever new information is added, a whole copy (or, at least, a segment long enough to ensure that the latest addition did not tamper with the pre-existing blockchain) is transmitted across the network.

Reason? Nobody will be able to alter enough copies of the blockchain to tamper with it (nobody will have 51%), e.g. to add further information upstream.

This obviously introduces other issues, e.g. across how many parties and holding how much votes should a network grow, in order to have the smallest size possible but still deliver its value, transparency, security?

You can find more details and discussions on Wikipedia[44] (including links).

Anyway, while closing this book, I received on Linkedin a reference to a paper written by Stanford students on machine-to-machine smart contracts using blockchain[45].

As many other proposals, the case discussed within the paper could actually be considered an incremental innovation.

Incremental, as focused on adding value using blockchain to existing activities and processes, not new concepts of mobility.

But it is anyway more structured than many business proposals and business case presentations I saw to push for the adoption of the blockchain.

In the future, as discussed e.g. by the study released by MIT[46] around the 20th anniversary of the publication of "The Machine that Changed the World"[47], individuals' mobility will change.

As each individual vehicle will be part of a completely different systemic approach, to enable a smart city to work smoothly- whatever propulsion system will bring us the future.

---

[44] https://en.wikipedia.org/wiki/Blockchain

[45] https://linkedin.com/feed/update/urn:li:activity:6490134148953489409 – contains both the link to the article, my commentary, and the original post I received the link from (retrieved on 2019-01-13)

[46] Mitchell - Reinventing the Automobile http://robertolofaro.com/books/suggested-readings/233-mitchell-reinventing-the-automobile-isbn-9780262013826-3-5-5

[47] https://www.librarything.com/work/220908/book/111584725

A Far West in the cloud: where is what?

When you read about the cloud, usually journalists are referring to companies moving their data and information technology online.

In reality, anybody using a mobile phone is on the cloud.

And even most of those using a computer and connecting to the Internet are already usually elements on the cloud.

For the time being, most smartphone users who own other devices or computers are used to do one task (or delegate it to their device): "synchronization", e.g. to ensure that the same contacts list is shared across all the devices.

Synchronization nowadays in reality means "duplication".

For the time being, we are still in A Far West in the cloud: where is what?

Moving toward a data-centric society requires making it as simple as possible to both access, share, and control data.

The next time you will buy something with your mobile, think about how many places are involved in completing that activity.

It is true that we are already in that condition described by Arthur Clarke: our technology is so complex but apparently so simple to use, that it seems as if things happen by magic.

When you add an application to your mobile phone, have a look at the authorizations that it requires.

The GDPR actually reduces complexity, as it defines common rules and a set of "natural" expectations.

It will take some time and, probably, some highly visible cases of violation, before it is really enforced.

But we already saw a change: companies collecting and storing data such as Facebook are now continuously reporting security issues that, in the past, would have been disclosed only by a third party.

Data are still distributed around, so a net result of the GDPR is now that websites that are "aggregator" of information from other websites (maybe to sell advertisement) are actually asking your consent.

And then transferring you to another website asking consent.

And then transferring to another website that....

So, the first step was tracking better who gets what, and the next will be instead to improve the level of consent.

If you want to access information that seems to be on the first website, and instead is on the third, and all three ask you to give consent, store cookies, and maybe even register, then obviously there are some further intuitive improvements.

Enforcing that streamlining would require anyway that all the information is linked via something akin to a blockchain.

Or: that information is traceable to its source, so that cookies and registrations can be automatically invalidated when obtained through deceit.

Is centralization of access really the future?

This chapter could have a second title: think before you act.

In a data-centric world, giving consent implies, for the time being, de facto opening the gate to reuses of your data.

Why not something similar in the future also for end citizens?

Install an app, and it could turn your smartphone or collection of devices into an "info consumer and data provider", maybe with some AI dropped in to help you reassess continuously how much you want or makes sense to share, and offsetting parts or all the operational costs

Example: if your routine brings you to have a regular pattern through areas where there are no sensors, adding a sensor for, say, pollution, or traffic monitoring, could actually generate value for providers.

Without their need to find a provider willing to set up physical permanent infrastructure that would provide the same service, and the smart contract could be set up via something as simple as answering to a questionnaire online about what is acceptable or not for you to share.

Thereafter, the system defines a "profile" and configures accordingly your devices with "data firewalls", and obtaining in exchange a segment of the value that you will receive

Anonymization is not a solution, as removing some elements of identification across multiple dimensions of analysis could still allow to assemble an identification.

Centralization of access is really the future?

Or are we just expanding the array of potential options?

Eventually, for those living in a urban location, probably having a computer at home storing data on a local hard disk would make not that much sense.

Computers at home or in your pocket, or even those that will be "embedded" in your clothing, accessories, or mobility devices will keep the data that will need to be re-used on the cloud-where synchronization becomes correlation.

Or: where data from a smartphone and data from e.g. your own fridge might merge with data from your banking account and your own grocery shopping list.

Much easier, and much more reliable, if you are always on, and your connection is fast and reliable, to store the data within the cloud.

Then, each one of your devices will access the cloud, and add or retrieve information as needed, except data that you do not need to store.

As for data that do not need to be stored on the cloud, might be stored within the cloud of your neighborhood.

Storing virtually at the edge, supporting something that is being done locally- data that will stay "on the edge".

When this will happen, it would be easier to do what I described before, i.e. having on your mobile devices an "automated consent/negotiation mechanism".

4 CONNECTING THE DOTS

As customary in this book series, this chapter would require a whole book.

But, instead, I prefer adding one-page sections that aim to raise awareness and potentially feed doubts.

The concept is the same that I discussed within the (free) fictional business case associated to the book on planning and change[48].

It is not the plan that you produce, but the planning exercise that matters.

And yes, it was an indirect quote from a famous WWII general.

---

[48] See https://robertolofaro.com/quplan

In the XXI century, complexity demands that we get used to connect knowledge, and identify reliable sources to keep ahead of trends, as discussed before in this book.

Otherwise you will be able to deliver at most incremental innovation, and at worst... reinvent a wheel when not needed.

Always remember Gresham Law[49]: bad knowledge, well presented, can easily filter out good knowledge presented in a way that only those "in the known" can understand.

Following my own advice, this introduction contains references to more "technical" sources on the bits and pieces needed to create a data-centric society.

First, I would like to share the concern expressed by others more technically qualified that myself about the excessive hype on 5G, IoT etc: *""In the last few years, in 5G, people are working on the radio side. Right now, when people start deploying, it's the mobile side," Li says [NDR: Richard Li chief scientist of future networks at Huawei and the chairman of the ITU Network 2030 group]. "But the fixed network side is still 4G. They do not match." Li is concerned that, with the emphasis on bringing 5G to fruition to deliver gigabit speeds to personal devices, the greater infrastructure has been neglected.*

The upshot is that while the larger amounts of data heralded by 5G will zip through edge infrastructure without delay, older, less advanced infrastructure could very well throttle that same data over longer distances."[50]

---

[49] https://en.wikipedia.org/wiki/Gresham's_law

[50] https://spectrum.ieee.org/tech-talk/telecom/internet/network-2030-wants-to-address-the-problems-5g-could-bring-to-our-communications-systems

Or: we risk a "much ado about nothing".

It will be anyway useful to have "Edge" data processing at 5G speeds, but until all the infrastructure is ready to seamlessly integrate the huge amount of data, we risk missing the real transformational potential of our 24/7 data-centric society.

Beside data, transactions, once devices have on board some "intelligence" helping them to manage consent and data exchange in real-time, as I wrote above.

A caveat: it is not just a matter of transmitting the data, it means also having within the infrastructure enough intelligence to decide if, when, how to transmit.

As an example of a complex structure and communication patterns in the late 1950s integrating multiple sources, see "The Power of Decision", a 1958 declassified documentary[51].

Now, that was a system including many manual "connectors" or "relays" of information- imagine instead something few orders of magnitude faster, and having to sort out what information is really relevant, and what is redundant.

If 100 people are watching the same football match in a specific location, does it make sense to "broadcast" one hundred times, or would it be enough to send it once to the nearest "Edge sub-community", so that all the infrastructure upstreams (fiber optic, etc.) is allocated just for 1/100th of the "dumb" approach?

But if interested, have a look at the article listed above.

Another item to consider is equally physical.

---

[51] https://www.youtube.com/watch?v=pmxz8Jr86tg

Yes, the IPv6[52] allows for more Internet-aware devices than IPv4, but we need to have something more than cheaper and more readily available "individual addresses" for each device.

We need also to have sensors so cheap that even a chocolate bar or a disposable packaging can have their own level of connectivity (no, it isn't a joke).

Therefore, another quest is to be able to create cheaper and smaller sensors, antennas, and overall electronics.

A recent article about connecting disposable objects presented the case for paper- and plastic-based sensors[53]- including a pricing analysis.

.So far, the items discussed are all focused on technology- but, as hinted in previous chapters, we are in also for a regulatory overhaul- more about this later.

Think again about the aeronautics industry: air traffic control rules defined for airplanes and vehicles generally taking-off from and landing in purpose-built facilities.

Recently, in order to protect from drones the airspace of civilian airport facilities in the UK, eventually the military had to install an Israeli systems that creates a "buffer" around a facility by taking over anything that enters the airspace

You can have tens or hundreds of low-cost drones flying around: no human could keep track of all of them.

---

[52] https://en.wikipedia.org/wiki/IPv6

[53] https://spectrum.ieee.org/semiconductors/materials/the-internet-of-disposable-things-will-be-made-of-paper-and-plastic-sensors

Another element that many consider a critical enabling factor for a data-centric society is the blockchain.

Reason? It enables not only keeping track of information, but having a decentralized way to have proof that data have not been tampered with in transmission- with no central authority.

The original implementation of the blockchain to transactions, bitcoin, not only consumes energy at a Gargantuan level of voracity, but also can "manage" small numbers of transactions involving a small amount of data.

Ethereum, another cryptocurrency, is more commonly associated with a potential further enabling factor (that per se would not require blockchain), smart contracts.

As reported by an article on a forthcoming improvement in energy consumption[54]: *"Ethereum mining consumes a quarter to half of what Bitcoin mining does, but that still means that for most of 2018 it was using roughly as much electricity as Iceland. Indeed, the typical Ethereum transaction gobbles more power than an average U.S. household uses in a day."*

The promise? To reduce energy consumption by 99%.

Other technologies? IoT, high and widespread availability of always faster networks, artificial intelligence, machine learning, and... whatever comes next.

The next few pages contain just outlines: further publications will follow in the future.

---

[54] https://spectrum.ieee.org/computing/networks/ethereum-plans-to-cut-its-absurd-energy-consumption-by-99-percent - the article contains also excerpts from an interview with the creator of Ethereum, Vitalik Buterin

Individuals in a data-centric society

In all this technological paraphernalia, many seem to forget that, in the end, we are talking about data generated by people, either directly or indirectly.

The economic value will be transferred in whatever form will make sense in the next few decades: in kind, services, time-saving streamlining of activities, etc.- not just money.

Think about it: having access to timely information that enables you to save on what you would anyway buy has already changed purchasing behaviors of many individuals.

The main element will be obviously avoiding a new form of "social exclusion", between those who would be able to extract value, and those who, lacking skills or means, will not.

In 2018 were already making the round of social networks pictures supposedly of street merchants and beggars in China showing a QR-code, from urban areas that are becoming cash-less.

Fake or true, highlight a potential that all of us technocrats and techno-enthusiasts routinely forget each time a new technological paradigm shift happens: we assume that what is normal for us is normal for everybody.

Also, individuals will be both people and, as discussed before, "circles of influence": from their own family or neighbors, to other levels of sub-communities, not necessarily joined by geography, creating new issues about concepts such as "jurisdiction" on transactions that would actually transform and generate data as they go.

The changing concept of infrastructure

Data-centric services for an "Internet everywhere society" turn data aggregation and maintenance of the infrastructure into a "common", i.e. a shared interest.

Over a decade ago, in order to expand access to the Internet faster, I was told by a colleague living there that in his town in Austria those keeping their connection open to others, and buying, to that end, a router, could offset connection costs.

It will increasingly become critical for all those aiming to be actively involved within society to be both consumers and producers of data, contributors to the future of open data.

Open data? Following the late 1990s push from e.g. the OECD to increase transparency and e-government services by publishing data, we are still in the first phases of the next evolution, where open data will not just be created by institutions, but also easily accessible and expandable with other sources, and you could talk of an "open data global infrastructure".

As an example, by expanding the limited experiments to use sensors in your car or smartphone to feed data to your community, so that there is no need to have additional sensors purchased or rented and maintained by your local authorities.

The real issue? Having an infrastructure smart enough to be able to detect and use autonomously open data when needed.

An environment for new products and services yet to be designed, as each new reuse of data will increase geometrically the potential for further connections and services.

Lowering complexity of continuous integration

Recently, whenever I heard the word "ecosystem", it sounded as if the supplier wanted exclusive access to customers- and "attract", as if by magic, other markets.

Interoperability has to be a key feature of a data-centric society, lowering the complexity of integration of new data.

Furthermore, no exclusivity of proprietary ecosystem, and regulatory anti-trust.

Probably the current portability and right to access embedded in GDPR will evolve, into the compulsory availability of an API at a nominal transactional cost for anybody willing to store and re-use data that require consent.

A new context, regulating not discrete transactions between two parties that use the integration between machines as intermediaries, but continuous interactions.

Interactions that generate further interactions with unforeseen third parties as a consequence of the data exchanged, being for the initiating party... just one transaction.

An old 1985 article from Jans Rasmussen[55] might be useful as a starting point for a brainstorming on the subject, without getting carried away from current technology, and focusing instead on key concepts[56].

---

[55] Hollnagel, Mancini, Woods (eds.) "Intelligent Decision Support in Process Environments", NATO ASI Series F Vol. 21, Springer-Verlag 1986

[56] Article available online http://orbit.dtu.dk/files/53754046/ris_m_2519.pdf

Edge computing as a citizens' right

Since the Internet was opened to the general public, there have been various requests to alter its governance.

To make it independent from the US Government, to introduce as a basic human right a degree of free access, etc.

Most of those demands have been accepted, and even enshrined in few Constitutions, but there is a new issue.

We have currently a dichotomy within the data infrastructure, as on radio and mobile we are converging to 5G, while the fiber and physical connections are at most on 4G[57].

Therefore, for a while we will have probably more data at the edge, citizen-to-citizen, and probably also have to create small sub-communities that will need to exchange data at 5G speed.

Providing edge-level storage and processing to citizens through a "standard" infrastructure would create additional value, as new concepts of services and integration with products could be generated at the local level, by "emergence" out of needs, i.e. demand not just driving, but designing offer.

Then this could evolve into virtual products (new services) that might actually be adopted/licensed by other communities (or even businesses), generating a return for the creating teams.

Hence, edge computing could enable grassroot services, a form of "civic hacking" accelerating data-centric applied R&D.

---

[57] https://spectrum.ieee.org/tech-talk/telecom/internet/network-2030-wants-to-address-the-problems-5g-could-bring-to-our-communications-systems

Judge and be judged

Web 2.0 brought about "likes" and "voting up/down", and other forms of interaction between customers and suppliers.

Eventually, with social networks, it became easy for everybody to interact with other customers (or bots).

Currently, most of the "approvals" expressed are confined within a specific community.

Say: Twitter, Facebook, Linkedin, Instagram, etc.

Or the other way around, notably for pre-Internet systems, e.g. credit scoring, or central government tax and compliance systems.

The new social credit system in China[58] that everybody is worrying about is more a case of the latter.

Eventually, similar systems will be adopted everywhere- as they are just an extension of existing systems (e.g. papers that allow or not to travel).

But in the future will gradually become bi-directional.

In a world where data are continuously exchanged automatically without any human intervention, it becomes critical not only to have visibility on who has access to what, but also remove unreliable counterparts as soon as possible- as discussed in the next section, on "social governance".

---

[58] https://en.wikipedia.org/wiki/Social_Credit_System

Toward social governance

The previous section discussed the social credit system.

Scary? Something worth of 1984?

Personally, I think that I would rather have a score assigned by a government subject to transparency and that can be sent home via elections, than a stateless company.

Social governance has been part of structured societies at least since states have been created with boundaries.

A data-centric society could be lost in details, and apply "penalty points" that are simply an inheritance of the old paper-based systems.

The alternative?

Moving from social engineering and social management to social governance, with a continuous re-assessment of what society considers to be "socially acceptable".

We already have laws that are linked to quantitative targets, notably within the European Union.

Probably data exchanges will enable a different kind of adjudication and court system, where for minor violations, instead of having a "trusted local", there will be a kind of "collective wisdom" with automated oversight, both speeding-up, de-clogging, and democratizing our court system.

Consequence? Collective oversight- within a framework of rules yet to define.

Swarming toward a data-centric society

I hold a EU passport, and I have been following European politics since I was 17, and saw how, on the supranational level, we are often used to highly technical agreements that, in reality, are nothing more than a convergence of interests.

Now, if you read the previous sections, you saw that, from a social, political, and also business perspective, personally I consider that a data-centric society will restructure our concepts e.g. of privacy, ownership, income, work, and, of course, law.

The key feature would be a potential "democratization", once we have in place an infrastructure that removes the technical complexity.

Then, we could actually consider the "convergence of interests" as something that will work at any level, and produce instantaneous rearrangements- as in a swarm[59].

We will be swarming our way toward a data-centric society, one network of interests at a time, as convergences of interests will create "trends", but trends will be overlapping.

Trends will generate services that will stay on only until sustainable: there will be no setup or infrastructure cost, there will be in most cases also no concept of "depreciation" or recovery of the initial investment.

As in the Amazon/Bezos credo- we could always be at day one.

---

[59] https://en.wikipedia.org/wiki/Swarm_behaviour

The end of the beginning

It can be said that this volume, as it is focused on a theme that covers various social, political, business, and technological issues, is an application of the framework discussed in the previous four volumes, all focused on change within a digital context.

There are four dimensions of analysis:

Actors: as there will be multiple roles in any transition, and a critical issue will be identifying the appropriate mix of talents to be involved across all the lifecycle of the initiative, from assessment of the current status, to definition of the target operating model, to phase-in of the changes and phase-out of the pre-existing organization, processes, and systems.

Methods: any cultural and social transformation, including digital transformation, require identifying the appropriate approach to be used- not just in terms of resource management and budget allocation, but also communication planning and stakeholder involvement (and manage externalities).

Means: while actors and methods define the human side of resources and stakeholders, the starting environment will involve physical and conceptual constraints; for a data-centric transformation, selecting relevant data is a must, to avoid both data scarcity and its counterpart, data hoarding.

Purposes: usually purposes are the starting point but, after restating the other three dimensions, it is possible to finalize the feasibility of a specific target scenario- and align purposes to the constraints identified for the other three dimensions.

A cross-reference to the other volumes of this series:

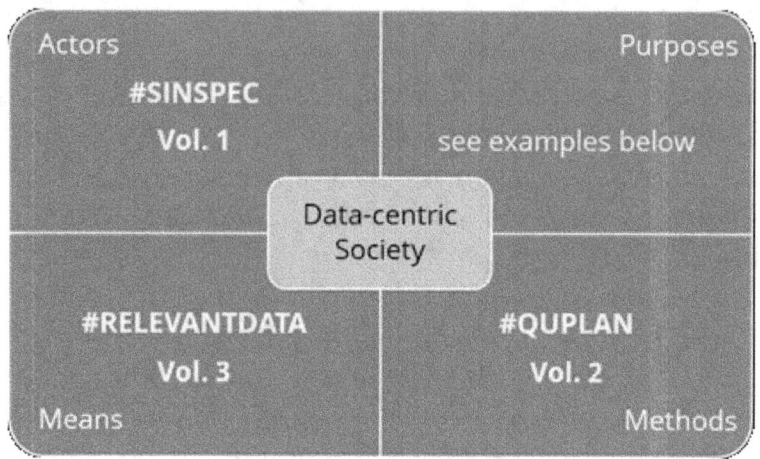

The following are few examples for the "purposes"[60]:

- on introducing innovation-related policies, a discussion of some times using Italy as a case study (2018):
  Just another book on innovation (in Italy) (vol. 4 of "Connecting the Dots") ISBN 978-1723163937

- on the impacts of the GDPR regulation (2018):
  The business side of GDPR: cultural and organizational impacts ISBN 978-1718910836

- on the use of private devices within a business environment, and associated data privacy issues (2014):
  The business side of BYOD: cultural and organizational impacts ISBN 978-1494844264

- on integrating online and offline communication for advocacy and political campaigning (2014, in Italian):
  Strumenti per la comunicazione e promozione di idee - #DirittoDiVoto – 01" ISBN 978-1505281521

---

[60] https://robertolofaro.com/ctr-books